HANDBOOK OF FUEL TECHNOLOGY AND ENERGY RESOURCES

BIOMASS CONVERSION TECHNOLOGIES

BIOENERGY AND BIOFUELS

FUEL TECHNOLOGY AND ENERGY RESOURCES

TABLE OF CONTENTS

1. INTRODUCTION 4
2. BIO-CHEMICAL CONVERSION 5
   - 2.1. ANAEROBIC DIGESTION 6
     - 2.1.1. MANURE STORAGE 7
     - 2.1.2. CROP STORAGE 7
     - 2.1.3. PRE-TREATMENT 8
     - 2.1.4. DIGESTER 8
     - 2.1.5. POST-DIGESTION STORAGE AND USE 8
     - 2.1.6. GAS ENGINE 8
     - 2.1.7. BIOMETHANE 9
   - 2.2. FERMENTATION IN THE PRODUCTION OF BIOETHANOL 9
3. THERMO-CHEMICAL CONVERSION 10
   - 3.1. COMBUSTION 13
     - 3.1.1. THE BIOMASS COMBUSTION PROCESS 13
     - 3.1.2. COMBUSTION EFFICIENCY 14
     - 3.1.3. SMALL-SCALE DOMESTIC COMBUSTION FOR HEAT 15
     - 3.1.4. MEDIUM-SCALE COMBUSTION FOR HEAT AND POWER 15
     - 3.1.5. BIOMASS CO-FIRING FOR ELECTRICITY 15
     - 3.1.6. EFFICIENCY CONSIDERATIONS IN COMBUSTION SYSTEMS. 16
   - 3.2. GASIFICATION 16
     - 3.2.1. THE GASIFICATION PROCESS 17
     - 3.2.2. GASIFICATION SYSTEMS 17
   - 3.3. PYROLYSIS 18
     - 3.3.1. FAST PYROLYSIS 20
     - 3.3.2. SYSTEMS INTEGRATION OF PYROLYSIS TECHNOLOGY 21
     - 3.3.3. PRODUCTS OF PYROLYSIS 22
     - 3.3.4. CATALYTIC UPGRADING OF BIO-OIL TO BIO-FUELS 24
4. PHYSIO-CHEMICAL CONVERSION 25

    4.1. PRODUCTION OF BIODIESEL FROM PALM FRUIT FEEDSTOCK 25
        4.1.1. EXTRACTION OF THE PALM OIL 26
        4.1.2. CONVERSION OF PALM OIL TO BIODIESEL 26

5. IMPORTANT FACTORS TO CONSIDER IN THE PRODUCTION OF BIOFUELS AND BIOENERGY 28
    5.1. FEEDSTOCK CONSIDERATIONS 28
    5.2. SCALE OF OPERATION 28
    5.3. PRE-PROCESSING TECHNOLOGIES 29
    5.4. CONCLUSION 29

1. INTRODUCTION

Biomass can be converted into several useful forms of energy using different processes. Fig. 1 portrays a number of different biomass (to bioenergy) conversion pathways. Various factors affect the choice of conversion process; these can include: the type, quantity, and characteristics of biomass feedstock, the desired form of the energy or end-use requirements, environmental standards, policy, economic conditions, and project-specific factors. In most situations, it is the form in which the energy is required and the feedstocks which are available that determine the appropriate process route.

Bioenergy is the term used to describe energy derived from biomass feedstocks. A number of stages (such as harvesting, drying, storage, transportation, processing, etc.) are required to convert biomass into a useful energy source. Conversion of biomass to energy is undertaken using three main process technologies: bio-chemical, thermo-chemical, and physio-chemical. Bio-chemical conversion encompasses two main process options: anaerobic digestion (AD) (production of biogas, a mixture of mainly methane and carbon dioxide) and fermentation (production of ethanol). Within thermo-chemical conversion, the four main process options are combustion, pyrolysis, and gasification. Physio-chemical conversion consists principally of extraction (with esterification) where oilseeds are crushed to extract oil. An over-view of each of the main energy conversion options is presented in the following sub-sections to provide an understanding of the technologies in the context of greenhouse gas (GHG) emissions.

The information here should provide sufficient background for students to be able to outline and understand the steps in a typical bioenergy conversion scheme. Sufficient numerical detail is given of yields and efficiencies.

For some processes, such as combustion, the conversion process directly releases the desired energy end-product. For other processes (such as fermentation) conversion results in an intermediate vector (in this case a liquid) which is then converted to provide energy. For some prime-movers, e.g. aero-engines, significant upgrading of the fuel may be required to meet appropriate standards and prevent damage. Those final conversion steps are often in boilers, engines, and turbines that have been adapted to the characteristics of the biomass-derived intermediate. It is important to note that the efficiency and performance of that final conversion step often varies for different vectors and it cannot be assumed, e.g. that pyrolysis oil will achieve the same combustion efficiency as fossilderived fuel oil or that the airborne emissions from syngas combustion will be the same as natural gas combustion. Wherever possible, primary data relating to the performance of the specific option being pursued should be used. If that is not available, carefully consider what factors might make a difference to the GHG balance of the overall system before using 'best-fit' data from a similar system and carrying out appropriate sensitivity checks.

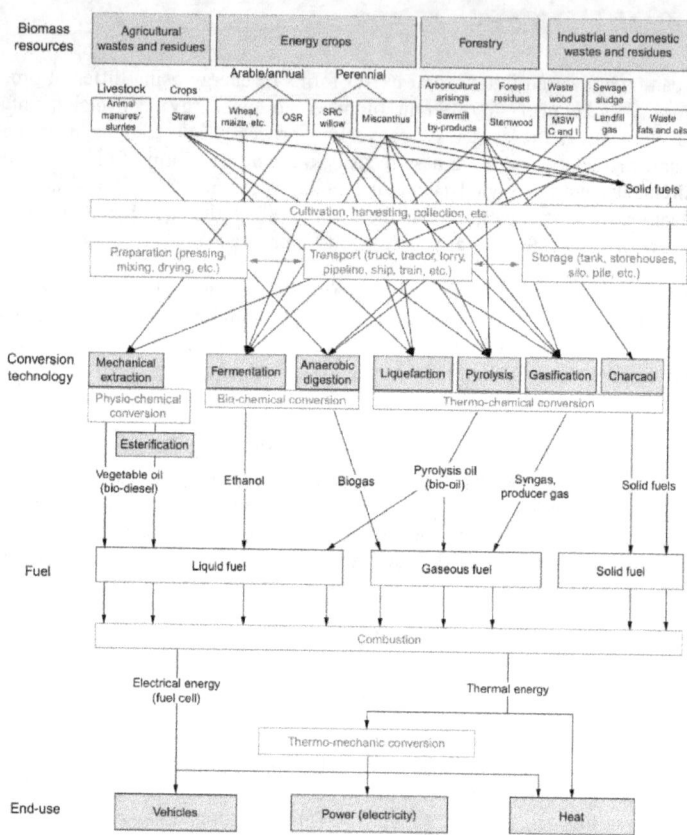

Fig. 1. Schematic representation of biomass conversion pathways.

2. BIO-CHEMICAL CONVERSION

Bio-chemical (or biological) conversion processes include both **Anaerobic Digestion (AD)** and **Fermentation (to produce bioethanol)**. AD utilises bacteria to transform the organic matter into gaseous products, offering reasonable economics and abundant applications worldwide. By comparison, fermenting the feedstock, yeasts are used to convert the contained sugar into bioethanol. This produces a diluted alcohol which then needs to be distilled and thus suffers from a lower overall process performance and high plant cost.

2.1. ANAEROBIC DIGESTION

AD is the conversion of organic material directly to a gas, known as biogas. Biogas is a mixture of mainly methane and carbon dioxide with small quantities of other gases such as hydrogen sulphide. Organic non-lignocellulosic (non-woody) material, the feedstock (also known as substrate) is converted by micro-organisms in the absence of oxygen. This conversion process produces stable and commercially useful compounds and is similar to composting except that composting is aerobic (involving oxygen) in its breakdown of organic matter. The biomass is converted by bacteria in an anaerobic environment, producing a gas with an energy content of about 20%–40% of the lower heating value (LHV) of the feedstock. AD is a commercially proven technology and is widely used for treating high moisture content (m.c.) organic wastes, i.e. 80%–90% m.c.

Feedstocks for AD include organic wastes and residues (such as animal manures or slurry) or energy crops (such as maize silage) grown specifically for feeding the AD plant. Anaerobic digesters produce conditions that encourage the natural breakdown of organic matter by bacteria in the absence of air. The two main products from an AD plant are:
- Biogas. This is a mixture of ~50%–60% methane, ~40%–50% carbon dioxide, and traces of other 'contaminant' gases;

- Bio-fertiliser (digestate). This is an inert and sterile wet product with valuable plant nutrients and organic humus. It can be separated into liquid and solid fractions for application to land or secondary processing.

AD produces biogas which can be combusted to generate electricity and/or heat or upgraded to biomethane and injected into the gas grid or used as a road fuel. It also provides a useful organic fertiliser as a by-product, making it an extremely promising technology with diverse applications. The generation of biogas is based on a complex process in various stages. Many factors influence the process from the cultivation of biomass, operating conditions, through to the end utilisation of the biogas. A schematic of a typical on-farm AD system showing the main on-site processes is presented in Fig. 2.

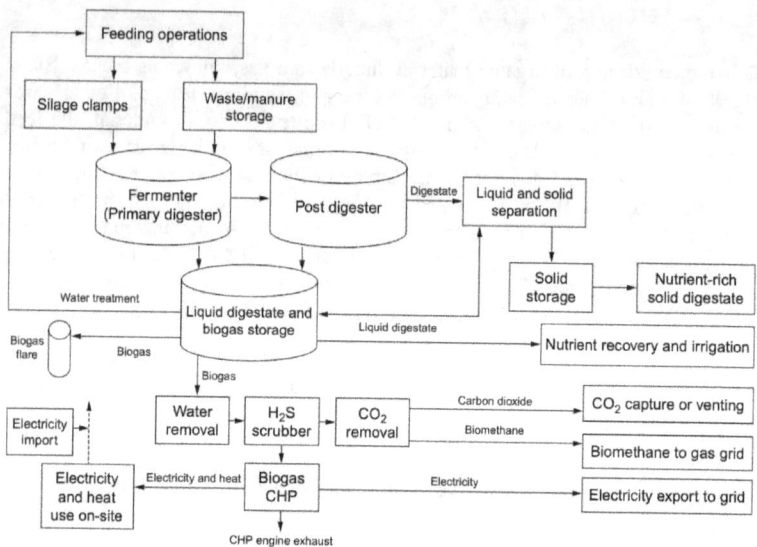

Fig. 2. Schematic overview of a typical farm-based AD system.

2.1.1. MANURE STORAGE

The most common manure storage systems are cellars, silos, and manure bags. Manure contains bacteria that will produce methane as soon as it is excreted. Methane production in storage is a source of GHG emissions and will lower the biogas yield of the digester. Therefore, it is important to transport manure from storage to the digester as soon as possible, which is generally done by means of a pump.

2.1.2. CROP STORAGE

The addition of other biomass (called a co-substrate) with a higher energy density than manure can substantially increase the biogas yield. Crop silage is generally stored in large clamps which store enough feedstock from the harvest to supply the digester for a year. Well-produced silage should only produce very negligible or zero GHG emissions. However, poorly made silage can suffer from losses and deteriorate, resulting in a higher requirement for feedstock and therefore increased GHG emissions from cultivation and harvesting.

2.1.3. PRE-TREATMENT

Essentially, there are three different methods for pre-treatment, depending on the type of co-substrate and the size characteristics as delivered to the AD plant: mechanical treatment, pre-heating, and thermal treatment. Some co-substrates require a size reduction, such as grinding or chopping, to prevent pieces of co-substrate that are too large for the pumps and mixers of the installation. Size reduction also increases the surface area for the bacteria, which will accelerate biogas production. Other types of co-substrate, such as fats, may require pre-heating in order to improve the flow characteristics. Certain co-substrates need thermal treatment in order to fulfil sanitation requirements.

2.1.4. DIGESTER

In the digester, the substrates are heated and the AD process takes place. Contents of the digester are stirred periodically to mix new substrate with the old substrate to improve the penetration of bacteria with the fresh substrate, to realise an even temperature in the digester, to prevent and disturb the build-up of sedimentary layers, and to improve the metabolism of the bacteria by removing the gas bubbles and replacing them with fresh feedstock. GHG emissions can arise from the digester only if gas can leak; generally modern digesters are gas-tight.

2.1.5. POST-DIGESTION STORAGE AND USE

Digested substrates (digestate) are normally stored in a post-digestion storage tank for subsequent use as organic fertiliser or recirculation in the AD system. Post-digesters also allow for additional biogas to be generated and captured. Liquid digestate is often used as a fertiliser and for irrigation, and there are several nutrient-recovery technologies available to increase the nutrient concentration. The solid digestate fraction can be used as a nutrient-rich soil improver.

Biogas produced in the digester requires storage until it can be used. The storage type will depend on the selected construction, but is usually stored either in the digester or an external gas storage unit. Modern larger biogas facilities have the ability to store biogas in both the post-digester and combined digestate and biogas storage tanks. Emissions from digestate or biogas storage can arise depending on the plant design and how the storage systems are managed.

2.1.6. GAS ENGINE

The gas engine, functioning as a combined heat and power (CHP) unit, uses the biogas to generate electricity and heat. Biogas electricity usually supplies the parasitic load of the AD facility with additional electricity generation exported to the grid. Produced heat will often be used to heat the digester and for pasteurisation with the remaining heat used for heating buildings, greenhouses, drying biomass, or for other industrial processes. Biogas can be used for generating heat only or can be processed for use as a transportation fuel or for supply to a natural gas grid.

2.1.7. BIOMETHANE

An alternative to combustion of raw biogas in CHP engines or boilers is the upgrading to a purer methane form known as biomethane. Upgrading biogas involves the removal of most of the carbon dioxide and further purification of other trace gases. Biomethane can then be used directly in vehicles with gas engines or injected into the gas grid. In terms of GHG emissions, biogas upgrading requires additional energy (usually electricity) and can require other inputs such as chemicals, water, or membranes depending on the upgrading technology employed. Methane emissions can also arise in the upgrading process. This increased energy requirement and methane loss can increase the GHG emissions from biomethane compared to biogas; however, it gives a more versatile high value fuel and can be used for a wider range of applications. Additionally, the carbon dioxide stream can be captured and used in industrial processes such as in greenhouses or the food and drinks industry. Methane slip (which increases fugitive GHG emissions) can be reduced to almost zero through the use of a thermal oxidiser. Production of biomethane can also have a nominally higher efficiency than biogas CHP since the electricity generation may waste heat; hence the use of Life Cycle Assessment (LCA) to assess and compare different conversion pathways is important.

2.2. FERMENTATION IN THE PRODUCTION OF BIOETHANOL

Fermentation is another anaerobic biological process with the simple sugars from biomass feedstock converted to alcohol and carbon dioxide by the action of a different set of microorganisms, usually yeasts. Ethanol (C_2H_5OH) is then separated from other components using heat to distill the mixture, so that the ethanol boils off and can then be cooled and condensed back to liquid. Fermentation is used commercially on a large-scale in various countries to produce ethanol from sugar crops (e.g. sugar cane, sugar beet) and starch crops (e.g. maize, wheat). The biomass is ground down and the starch converted by enzymes to sugars, with yeast then converting the sugars to cellular energy and thereby producing ethanol. Purification of ethanol by distillation is an energy-intensive step which can result in relatively low net energy balances with about 450L of ethanol being produced per ton (t) of dry corn. Solid residues produced from the fermentation process can be used as cattle-feed, and in the case of sugar cane, the bagasse can be used as a fuel for boilers or for subsequent gasification.

Bio-based ethanol (bioethanol) is most commonly used as an extender in petrol (gasoline) containing a percentage of ethanol. Higher blends (typically 85% ethanol, 15% gasoline— designated E85) are used in 'flexible-fuel vehicles' (FFVs) in countries such as Australia, Sweden, the United States, and Brazil. Perhaps the best known example of fermentation for fuel is the production of ethanol from sugar cane in Brazil where many cars run on 100% bioethanol. Sugar cane stalks contain sufficiently high amounts of sugar and the plant is currently the lowest cost source of producing ethanol. Maize (also known as corn) is the second largest source of bio-fuel feedstock today, primarily because of its dominance in the United States for ethanol production. Producing ethanol from grain starches requires more land than sugar cane, because the crops have lower fuel yields per hectare. The main sources of feedstock for fermentation in the Europe are wheat and sugar beet. Both of these crops are grown for food purposes and there are not significant surpluses available; hence fermentation is not anticipated to be used for bioenergy production on a large-scale in many parts of the world. However, fermentation can also be used as a pathway to a wide variety of products in a biorefinery, which can replace fossil fuel hydrocarbons in conventional refineries and there are significant research efforts to progress advanced technologies to enable fermentation of lignocellulosic feedstocks by pre-treatment and/or identification of appropriate enzymes.

3. THERMO-CHEMICAL CONVERSION

Thermo-chemical conversion of biomass can occur via **pyrolysis, gasification,** and **combustion**. Pyrolysis is the preliminary stage of all thermo-chemical processes since it comprises chemical reactions to form solid, liquid, and gaseous products without oxygen. Technologies that produce gaseous or liquid intermediate products that can be upgraded to higher value energy (transportation fuels, electricity, etc.) are particularly valuable. The main processes, the intermediate energy carriers, and the final energy products resulting from thermo-chemical conversion are illustrated in Fig. 3.

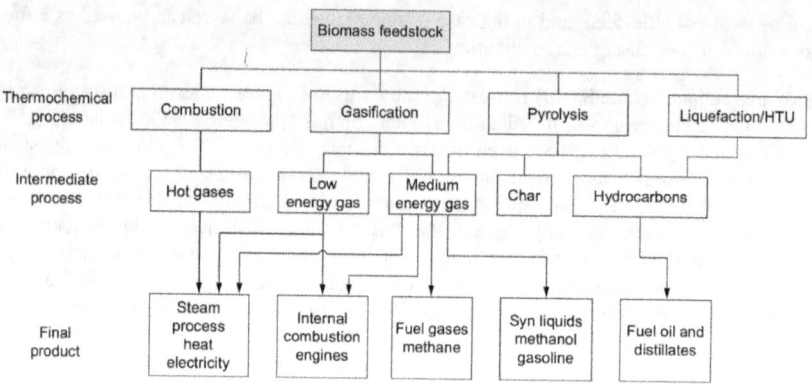

Fig. 3. Main processes, intermediate energy carriers and final energy products from the thermo-chemical conversion of biomass.

In general, thermo-chemical processes have higher efficiencies than bio-chemical/biological processes, quicker reaction times (a few seconds or minutes for thermochemical processes compared to several days, weeks, or longer for bio-chemical processes), and the superior ability to destroy most of the organic compounds, e.g. lignin materials in biomass are typically considered to be non-fermentable and consequently cannot be completely decomposed via biological approaches, whereas they are decomposable via thermo-chemical approaches.

As shown in Fig. 1. and Fig. 3., the stored energy contained within biomass can be released either directly as heat via combustion/co-firing, or could be transformed into solid (e.g. charcoal), liquid (e.g. bio-oils), or gaseous (e.g. synthetic gas) fuels via pyrolysis, liquefaction, or gasification with various utilisation purposes. Table 1 summarises the different types of thermo-chemical conversion processes, their classification, process conditions, and typical product yields.

Table 1. **Overview of Biomass Thermo-chemical Conversion Technologies**

Conversion Technology	Process Condition	Reactor Types	Product Yield		
			Liquid (wt.%)	Gas (wt.%)	Solid (wt.%)
Combustion	Maximum temperature: 740–1300°C, Air mass flow: 0.1–0.5 kg/m^2 s	Fixed bed combustor Fluidised bed combustor Circulating bed combustor Entrained flow bed combustor	Gas yield (m^3 gas/kg biomass): 1–2.6		
Gasification	Moderate to high temperature (600–1200°C), presence/absence of catalyst, small particle size desirable, gasifying agent	Fixed bed gasifier Moving bed gasifier Fluidised bed gasifier Entrained flow gasifier	Power and heat		
Fast Pyrolysis	Atmospheric pressure, small particle size (<3mm), short residence time (0.5-2s), moderate temperature (400-550°C), in the absence of oxygen	Fixed bed reactor Tubular reactor Bubbling fluidised bed reactor Circulating fluidised bed reactor	65 - 75	13 - 25	12 - 19
Slow Pyrolysis	Low heating rate, moderate temperature (350-750°C), atmospheric pressure, long residence time in absence of oxygen	Ablative Pyrolyzer Rotating Cones reactor Auger reactor Cyclone reactor (N.B. the reactor type that can be used will depend on the pyrolysis method)	30 - 50 in 2 phases	15 - 30	30 - 60
Intermediate Pyrolysis	Moderate temperature (<500°C), moderate vapor residence time (4-10s) and atmospheric pressure		45 - 55 in 2 phases	25 - 35	15 - 25
Flash Pyrolysis	Rapid heating (<0.5s), very small particle sizes (<0.5mm), temperature (400-1000°C)		60 - 70	10 -15	15 - 25
Vacuum Pyrolysis	Moderate temperature (300-500°C), pressure below atmospheric (<50kPa)		45 - 60	17 - 27	19 - 27
Ablative Pyrolysis	Moderate temperature (450-600°C), atmospheric pressure, particle size <3.5mm		60 - 80	6 - 10	12 - 20

3.1. COMBUSTION

Biomass has been burnt for heat since pre-historic times and it remains the most commonly used source of renewable energy in the world. A vast range of technologies are used from simple batch-operated designs in domestic homes to complex biomass-fired power stations with flue gas clean-up. This section describes the fundamental process involved in biomass combustion, the types of emissions evolved from combustion, and considerations around feedstock types. An overview is given of typical combustion systems at both domestic and large-scale power generation.

Biomass combustion is the simplest thermo-chemical conversion technology that takes place in the presence of air. Heat, power, or CHP are the main products of direct combustion of biomass; this process consists of consecutive heterogeneous and homogeneous reactions. Biomass combustion essentially depends on the particle size and properties of the feed- stock, temperature, and combustion atmosphere. High emissions of NO_x, CO_2, and particulate matter, in addition to ash handling, make combustion environmentally challenging.

3.1.1. THE BIOMASS COMBUSTION PROCESS

Combustion can be split into four stages: (1) drying, (2) pyrolysis, (3) volatiles combustion, and (4) char combustion. These stages are shown in Fig. 4.

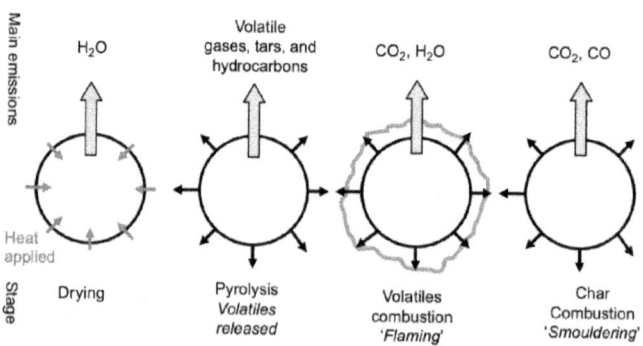

Fig. 4. Biomass combustion stages

A wide range of biomass sources can be considered for combustion including wood chips, wood pellets, and wood sourced directly by the user including scrub and waste woods. Adherence to strict fuel quality parameters is required for large-scale systems. Fuel types for domestic use are often more varied and the quality is not consistent, leading to wide variation in emissions levels. The best quality fuels contain high amounts of carbon and hydrogen and low amounts of other elements such as oxygen, nitrogen, sulphur, and trace elements. Nitrogen and sulphur species are associated with undesirable gaseous emissions. Trace elements such as potassium and sodium can lead to fouling within the combustion system, whereas chlorine leads to corrosion and silica causes excessive wear to milling equipment. Biomass typically contains higher levels of oxygen than coal or other fossil fuels. The fuel energy content (calorific value) is inversely proportional to the amount of oxygen present. A typical range of calorific values are shown in Table 2.

Table 2. **Typical Biomass Analysis and Calorific Values. Dry Basis Values.**

	Wood Pellet	Mixed Hardwood Chips	Waste Wood	MSW
Ash wt.%	1.10	0.93	3.23	16.82
Volatile wt.%	83.00	83.41	77.57	72.60
Fixed carbon wt.%	15.90	15.66	19.20	10.58
Gross calorific value MJ/kg	17.19	19.27	19.52	20.48

The first stage of combustion requires heat to dry the moisture; hence, it is desirable to have fuels with the minimal moisture content. Fresh wood chips can contain 50% moisture, whereas leaves can be over 90% water, which would not be easily combustible. Most stoves and boilers recommended biomass has less than 20% moisture content. Higher levels affect the combustion efficiency and increase the amount of smoke emitted.

3.1.2. COMBUSTION EFFICIENCY

The efficiency of a combustion system is related to how completely the fuel is burnt. The maximum emissions of CO_2 for a given mass of fuel will correlate to the maximum extraction of energy from the fuel because CO_2 is the final product of complete combustion. The presence of CO, volatile fuel fragments, and soot indicate lower combustion efficiency. The most efficient combustion systems are those where there is sufficient flow of air for complete combustion, which is always more than the stoichiometric fuel air ratio. The excess air is typically between 5% and 50%, depending on the combustor design and fuel properties. The combustion efficiency of a domestic fireplace might only be 20%–30%, whereas around 75% is achievable for a larger furnace system.

3.1.3. SMALL-SCALE DOMESTIC COMBUSTION FOR HEAT

The size, design, and complexity of a domestic system will affect the amount of pollutants produced. Designs include overfed, underfed, and moving grate systems. Batch-fed designs are typically fireplaces or stoves for radiant room heat. Fuels for batch-fed domestic use are generally logs and briquettes, although waste wood pieces are also commonly used. Continuously fed systems use wood chips or wood pellets—the latter being less likely to block the fuel feed system but more expensive.

3.1.4. MEDIUM-SCALE COMBUSTION FOR HEAT AND POWER

There are many examples of the use of wood chips or waste-derived fuels at district scale for provision of heat and/or power using conventional combustion technology. The efficiency of the system is dependent on the scale of application and associated steam conditions. It should be noted that CHP systems are usually designed to operate to service a particular heat demand. Some facilities can be operated even when that heat demand is lower or absent, but usually this will have a significant impact on the efficiency of the plant. It is therefore important to take into account the heat demand in the assessment as this may affect the number of hours for which a facility is run. If frequent start-ups are then required, the airborne pollutants may be higher during the start-up phase than the routinely reported steady state figures, making it difficult to accurately assess the lifetime impact.

3.1.5. BIOMASS CO-FIRING FOR ELECTRICITY

Biomass co-firing with coal has been commonly deployed across Europe and North America to encourage the de-carbonisation of electricity production. It is a relatively low-cost technology for efficiently and cleanly converting lignocellulosic biomass to electricity. During co-firing, the primary fuel (coal) is partially substituted by biomass in a high efficiency boiler. Depending on the boiler capacity and efficiency, the percentage of biomass co-firing varies between 5 and 20% by weight. The substitution of biomass reduces both GHG emissions from coal combustion and also produces lower amounts of NO_x and SO_x. Co-firing takes the advantage of the power plant's economies of scale and saves fossil fuels. Biomass can be burned in fixed bed combustors with thermal outputs of 1 MW$_{th}$ or larger.

3.1.6. EFFICIENCY CONSIDERATIONS IN COMBUSTION SYSTEMS

The efficiency of a boiler combustion process is assessed by how much energy from the fuel is transferred to the water for either heating or to produce electricity. Common sources of process inefficiency are heat loses via flue gases, convection and radiation to surroundings, and losses due to incomplete combustion of the fuel. A comparison of the combustion efficiencies for a pellet boiler and similarly sized oil and gas boilers is shown in Table 3. It can be seen that the lowest efficiency is given by the biomass pellet boiler, which has a corresponding high level of PM$_{10}$ particulate emissions. This indicates very poor levels of combustion, which could be improved by better air/fuel mixing, higher combustion temperatures, or a longer residence time for the fuel.

Table 3. **Comparison of Combustion Efficiency**

	Pellet Boiler (15kW)	Oil (15.5kW)	Natural Gas (15kW)
Efficiency/ %	75.0	89.5	99.0
PM10/ mg/Nm^3	47.6	60.0	0:3

3.2. GASIFICATION

The gasification process thermo-chemically converts an organic feedstock (e.g. liquid or solid fuel) into its gaseous components which depend on the gasification temperature. Strictly speaking, synthesis gas or syngas is only $H_2 + CO$ which is primarily formed at higher gasification temperatures (above 1200°C). At lower gasification temperatures, product gas is formed comprising CO, H_2, CH_4, and CO_2 and may include tar compounds which adversely affect gasification performance and downstream end-uses. Tar and ash are potentially produced as by-products which may have added value and provide different accounting routes for GHG emissions during gasification. In a well-designed gasifier, char is not normally a by-product. In practice, however, a small amount of char may be produced which represents inefficient gasification. The gasification efficiency can be expressed as the % conversion of carbon. Syngas and producer gas (for convenience now referred to collectively as syngas) can be used to produce heat, power, and chemical products. Historically, both wood and coal have been gasified to produce convenient gaseous fuel (syngas) for many applications worldwide, but have not been commercially sustained due to low-cost fossil oil and natural gas availability.

Gasification produces a flexible energy source. There is potential to produce heat via combustion in a boiler, electricity via combustion in reciprocating engines or gas turbines, or converted to a liquid bio-fuel, or substitute natural gas (SNG) for injection into gas grids.

3.2.1. THE GASIFICATION PROCESS

There are many different designs of modern gasifiers, but, during the process of gasification, woody biomass undergoes three distinct transitions. Firstly, wood is dehydrated before temperatures exceed 200°C, at which point gasification is initiated and char and vapours are produced. The presence of O_2 partially oxidises the char and vapours resulting in a gas containing CO, H_2, CO_2, and water as well as tars, ammonia, sulphur, and other impurities. A key parameter is the cold gas efficiency of the gasifier, which expresses the chemical energy in the outlet gas as a proportion of the chemical energy and sensible heat input to the gasifier. Cold gas efficiency will vary with gasifier design, scale, and conditions and is sensitive to the equivalence ratio (air flow rate/airflow for stoichiometric conditions).

Broadly speaking gasifiers can be classified in terms of their bed and gas flow direction, e.g. fixed bed (downdraft, updraft, or crossdraft), entrained flow, fluidised bed, or circulating bed. An oxidant is supplied to the combustion zone at typically 1/5 of the stoichiometric combustion ratio. Many gasifiers use catalysts (e.g. dolomite- or Ni-based) for catalytic steam reforming or partial oxidation of tars, or to enable catalytic upgrading to liquid bio-fuels. Often the catalytic process is done downstream from the gasifier after sufficient gas cleaning and composition adjustments. Mass flows of catalysts, their potential recovery and impact on product output, and GHG emissions need consideration. Downdraft gasifiers are suitable for small scale operation, typically from 10 to 250 kWe; there are MW systems out there, fluidised bed systems typically operate between a few MWe to 100MWe, and entrained flow from about 50 MWe to 1 GWe.

3.2.2. GASIFICATION SYSTEMS

To allow informed comparison between LCA of different gasifier designs and plants, system boundaries should generally include the impact of feedstock production, feedstock pre-processing or pre-treatment, the gasification system (including gas clean-up), and end utilisation of the syngas. The mass-flow and end-use of by-products, such as ash and biochar (see above), should be considered realising that their quality, quantity, and end-use will de- pend on the biomass feed characteristics, operational temperature profile, and residence time during the gasification process and gasifier design. The end-use of the syngas is largely deter- mined by the plant's scale and end demand. Power generation can be achieved by co-firing, CHP or, for larger plants, Integrated Gasification Combined Cycle (IGCC). In IGCC, gas turbines are used due to their higher thermal efficiencies, but the inlet gas temperature and pressure have to be optimised and to match the turbine design (e.g. 400–500°C and 5–20 bar). Plant lifetime may be increased by ensuring complete tar cracking, tar removal, or careful temperature control to avoid tar condensation within the plant. In some circumstances, process efficiency can be increased by burning a tar-laden gas. End emissions from the plant should be minimised by gasification optimisation. Process inputs to the gasification plant, e.g. gas clean-up technology (e.g. scrubbing, cyclonic, electrostatic precipitation, plasma) will require additional energy, resulting in other GHG contributions that require accounting.

The sustainable available biomass feedstock is increasingly being dominated by waste-derived and residual materials including municipal solid waste (MSW) or refuse-derived fuel (RDF), a refined version of MSW. These are capable of reducing GHG emissions with less stress on land usage when waste products (e.g. agricultural and domestic) are used as the feedstock compared to energy crops. However, such feedstocks present technical challenges to gasification plants, e.g. RDF may contain 20% plastics.

Syngas can be directly combusted for electricity generation, but it is more common for it to be purified, as then almost any hydrocarbon compound may be synthesised from it, including premium fuels such as methanol, ethanol, methane, and transport fuels. The first stage in this synthesis is to adjust the proportions of H_2 and CO to the ratio required in the desired product. For example, methanol is CH_3OH, and therefore needs two H_2 molecules for each CO converted. Using the Fischer-Tropsch process, syngas from biomass has been successfully converted to synthetic diesel. Additionally, the hydrogen which can be isolated from syngas has been used to power hydrogen fuel cells for the generation of electricity and to power electric vehicles. However, these purification steps are costly and energy-intensive, and efficiency needs to be improved if they are to become widely used. In addition to the challenges which face purification of syngas, the implementation of gasification is limited because of the initial feedstock requirements. Moisture and ash content, homogeneity, particle size, bulk density, and energy content must all be tightly controlled if gasification is to be efficient and this has limited uptake of the technology.

3.3. PYROLYSIS

Pyrolysis has become of major interest due to the flexibility in operation, versatility of the technology, and adaptability to a wide variety of feedstocks and products. Pyrolysis operates in anaerobic conditions where heat is usually provided externally and the constituents of biomass are thermally cracked to gases and vapours which usually undergo secondary reactions, thereby giving a broad spectrum of products. The conditions and circumstances that can have a major impact on the products and the process performance include feedstock, technology, reaction temperature, additives, catalysts, hot vapour residence time, solids residence time, and pressure.

Pyrolysis is the thermal decomposition of biomass occurring in the absence of oxygen, converting biomass to liquid (usually called bio-oil), solid, and gaseous fractions with various chemical reactions of feedstock. Lower process temperatures and longer hot vapour residence times favour the production of charcoal. Higher temperatures and longer residence times increase biomass conversion to gas, and moderate temperatures and short hot vapour residence time are optimum for producing liquids. Three products are always produced, but the proportions can be varied over a wide range by adjustment of the process parameters. Table 4 and Fig. 5. indicate typical product distribution obtained from different modes of pyrolysis, showing the considerable flexibility achievable by changing process conditions. Fast pyrolysis for liquids production is currently of particular interest commercially as the liquid can be stored and transported and used for energy, transport fuels, chemicals, or as an energy carrier.

Table 4. Typical Product Weight Yields (Dry Wood Basis) Obtained by Different Modes of
Pyrolysis of Wood

Mode	Conditions	Liquid	Solid	Gas
Fast	~500°C. Short hot vapour residence time <2 s	75 wt.% (bio-oil)	12 wt.% char	13 wt.%
Intermediate	~500°C. Moderate hot vapour residence time 5–30 s	50 wt.% in 2 phases	25 wt.% char	25 wt.%
Carbonisation (slow)	~400°C. Long hot vapour residence time hours → days	30 wt.% in 2 phases	35 wt.% char	35 wt.%
Gasification (allothermal)	~750–900°C. Moderate hot vapour time 5 s + in	3 wt.%	1 wt.% char	96 wt.%

FUEL TECHNOLOGY AND ENERGY RESOURCES

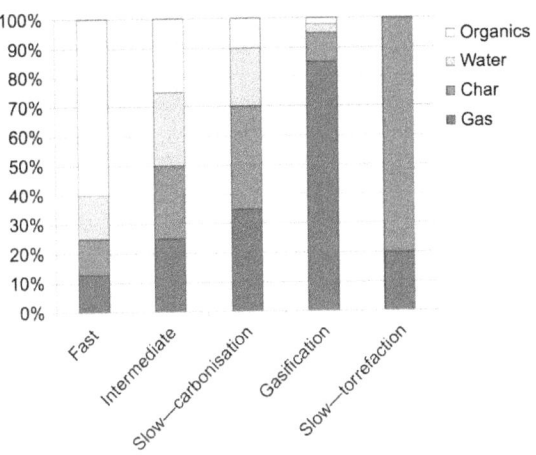

Fig. 5. Product spectrum from pyrolysis.

3.3.1. FAST PYROLYSIS

In fast pyrolysis, biomass decomposes very quickly to generate mostly vapours and aerosols and some charcoal and gas. After cooling and condensation, a dark brown homogenous mobile liquid is formed which has a heating value about half of that of conventional fuel oil. This is referred to as bio-oil. A high yield of liquid is obtained with most low ash biomass. Yields of up to 75 wt.% on dry biomass feed can be achieved.

The essential features of a fast pyrolysis process for producing liquids are:

- Small particle sizes of typically less than 5 mm for high heating rates and rapid devolatilisation,
- Feed moisture content of less than 10 wt.% since all the feed water reports to the liquid phase along with water from the pyrolysis reactions,
- Very high heating rates and very high heat transfer rates at the biomass particle reaction interface. This usually requires a finely ground biomass feed of typically less than 3 mm as biomass generally has a low thermal conductivity. The rate of particle heating is usually the rate-limiting step. Preparation of the biomass

(comminution, drying, and grinding) to this specification before pyrolysis needs to be considered in the overall process scheme.

- Carefully controlled pyrolysis reaction temperature of around 500°C to maximise the liquid yield for most biomass,
- Short hot vapour residence times of typically less than 2 s to minimise secondary reactions,
- Rapid removal of product char to minimise cracking of vapours, • Rapid cooling of the pyrolysis vapours to give the bio-oil product.

As fast pyrolysis for liquids occurs in a few seconds or less, heat and mass transfer processes and phase transition phenomena, as well as chemical reaction kinetics, play important roles. The critical issue is to bring the reacting biomass particles to the optimum process temperature as quickly as possible and minimise both their exposure to lower temperatures that favours formation of charcoal and their exposure to higher temperatures that accelerates thermal cracking. One way this objective can be achieved is by using small particles, for example, in the fluidised bed processes. Another possibility is to transfer heat very fast only to the particle surface that contacts the heat source which is used in ablative pyrolysis.

3.3.2. SYSTEMS INTEGRATION OF PYROLYSIS TECHNOLOGY

A conceptual fast pyrolysis process is depicted in Fig. 6. from biomass feed to collection of a liquid product. Each process step has several alternatives such as the reactor and liquid collection, but the underlying principles are similar. At the heart of a fast pyrolysis process is the reactor. The rest of the fast pyrolysis process consists of biomass reception, storage and handling, biomass drying and grinding, product collection, storage and, when relevant, upgrading. A typical biomass feed specification is up to 10% moisture and so drying and grinding are key steps from an LCA mass-energy balance perspective.

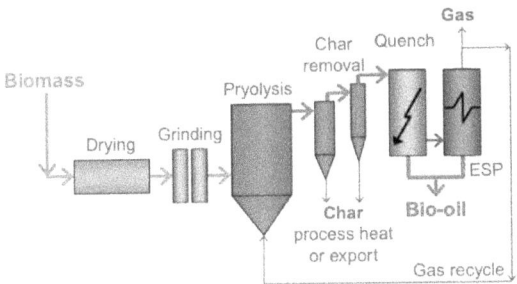

Fig. 6. Conceptual fast pyrolysis process.

3.3.3. PRODUCTS OF PYROLYSIS

3.3.3.1. Liquid Bio-oil

Liquid bio-oil is formed by rapidly quenching and thus 'freezing' the intermediate products of flash degradation of hemicellulose, cellulose, and lignin. The liquid, thus, contains many reactive species, which contribute to its unusual attributes. Pyrolysis oil typically is a dark brown, free-flowing liquid and approximates to biomass in elemental composition (Table 5). It is composed of a very complex mixture of oxygenated hydrocarbons with an appreciable proportion of water from both the original moisture and reaction product. Some solid char may also be present. Typical organics yields from different feedstocks and their variation with temperature is shown in Fig. 7. Liquid yield depends on biomass type, temperature, hot vapour residence time, char separation, and biomass ash content, the last two having a catalytic effect on vapour cracking. It is important to note that maximum yield is not the same as maximum quality, and quality needs careful definition if it is to be optimised.

Table 5. Typical Properties of Fast Pyrolysis Bio-oil

Physical Property	Typical Value
Moisture content	25%
pH	2.5
Specific gravity	1.20
Elemental analysis	
C	56%
H	6%
O	38%
N	0% - 0.1%
HHV as produced	17 MJ/kg
Viscosity (40°C and 25% water)	40 - 100 MPAs
Solids (char)	0.1%
Vacuum distillation residue	Up to 50%

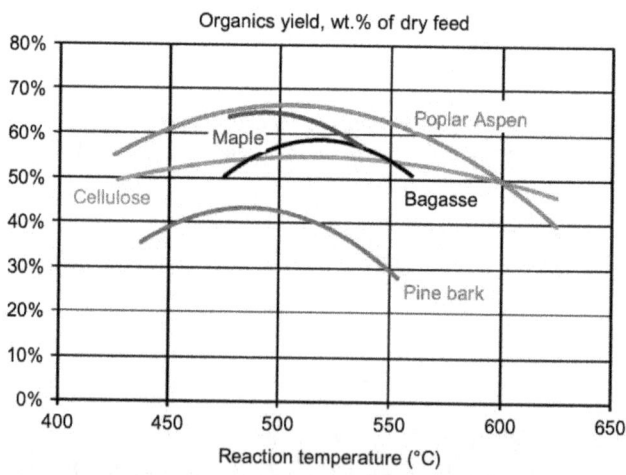

Fig. 7. Organics yield from different feedstocks.

The liquid contains varying quantities of water, which forms a stable single-phase mixture, ranging from about 15wt.% to an upper limit of about 30–50wt.% water, depending on the feed material, how it was produced, and subsequently collected. As stated above, a typical feed material specification is a maximum of 10% moisture in the dried feed material, as both this feed moisture and the water of reaction from pyrolysis, typically about 12% based on dry feed, report to the liquid product. Pyrolysis liquids can tolerate the addition of some water, but there is a limit to the amount of water which can be added to the liquid before phase separation occurs; in other words, the liquid cannot be dissolved in water. Water addition reduces viscosity, which is useful; reduces heating value which means that more liquid is required to meet a given duty; and can improve stability. The effect of water is therefore complex and important. Bio-oil is miscible with polar solvents such as methanol, acetone, etc., but totally immiscible with petroleum-derived fuels. This is due to the high oxygen content of around 35–40wt.%, which is similar to that of biomass, and provides the chemical explanation of many of the characteristics reported. Removal of this oxygen by upgrading requires complex catalytic processes which are described in the next sub-sections.

3.3.3.2. Char and Gas

Char and gas are by-products, typically containing about 25% and 5% of the energy in the feed material, respectively. The pyrolysis process itself requires about 15% of the energy in the feed, and of the by-products, only the char has sufficient energy to provide this heat. The heat can be derived by burning char in an orthodox reaction system design such as a circulating fluid bed, which makes the process energy self-sufficient and results in a high temperature flue gas. As the ash in the biomass is substantially retained in the char, and thereby concentrated, combustion needs careful control. This is practiced commercially. There are many other ways of providing the heat for pyrolysis, but in-process combustion of char is currently preferred. The waste heat from char combustion and any heat from surplus gas or by-product gas can be used for feed drying and, in large installations, could be used for export or power generation.

An important principle of fast pyrolysis is that a well-designed and well-run process should not produce any emissions other than clean flue gas, i.e. CO_2 and water, although they will have to meet local emissions standards and requirements.

3.3.4. CATALYTIC UPGRADING OF BIO-OIL TO BIO-FUELS

Upgrading bio-oil to a conventional transport fuel such as diesel, gasoline, kerosene, methane, and LPG requires full deoxygenation and conventional refining, which can be accomplished either by integrated catalytic pyrolysis or by decoupled liquid phase hydrodeoxygenation.

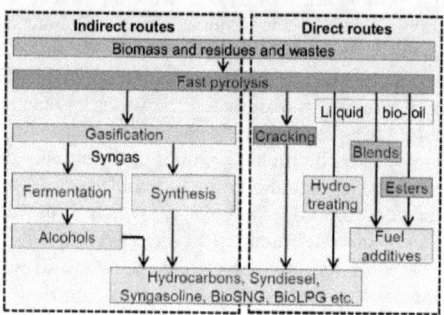

Fig. 8. Overview of fast pyrolysis upgrading methods.

4. PHYSIO-CHEMICAL CONVERSION

Physio-chemical conversion, also referred to as mechanical extraction, is a mechanical (physical) conversion process used to produce oil from the seeds of various biomass crops, such as oilseed rape (OSR), palm fruits and linseed. This process provides a liquid fuel which can undergo a further stage, known as esterification, which turns the oil to fatty acid methyl ester, more widely known as bio-diesel. The process produces not only oil, but also a residual solid or 'cake', which is suitable for animal fodder. This technology is used on a wide scale in Europe using vegetable oils from crops, primarily OSR, but waste fats and oils are also used. The main use of bio-diesel is as a liquid transport fuel; most commonly blended with diesel derived from petroleum.

4.1. PRODUCTION OF BIODIESEL FROM PALM FRUIT FEEDSTOCK

Palm oil is composed of 43% palmitic acid (C16, saturated fats), 37% oleic acid (C18, mono-unsaturated fats) and 9% linoleum acid (C18, poly-unsaturated fats). To produce palm oil, the palm fruit is first harvested from the tree. An average fresh fruit bunch weighs about 20 - 30kg and contains 1500 - 2000 fruits. The fruits are then treated with steam in a process known as sterilisation, This treatment inhibits the activities of enzymes in the fruit that may degrade the oil. Sterilisation also makes the stripping of the fruits from the bunches easier.

4.1.1. EXTRACTION OF THE PALM OIL

The stripping process involves the separation of the fruits from the bunch. This is achieved by mechanical means. The bunches are fed to a drum stripper, which rotates causing detachment of the fruits from the bunches. After stripping, the fruits pass through a screw press, which generates a mixture of oil, water and solids (fibre, mainly cellulose). The mixture of oil, water and solids from the screw press is separates in vibrating screens and clarification tanks. Vibrating screens remove some of the solids, while the rest of the solids and water is removed in the clarification tank. The palm oil is separated from the top of the clarification tank. After clarification, the residual moisture of the oil is removed by drying.

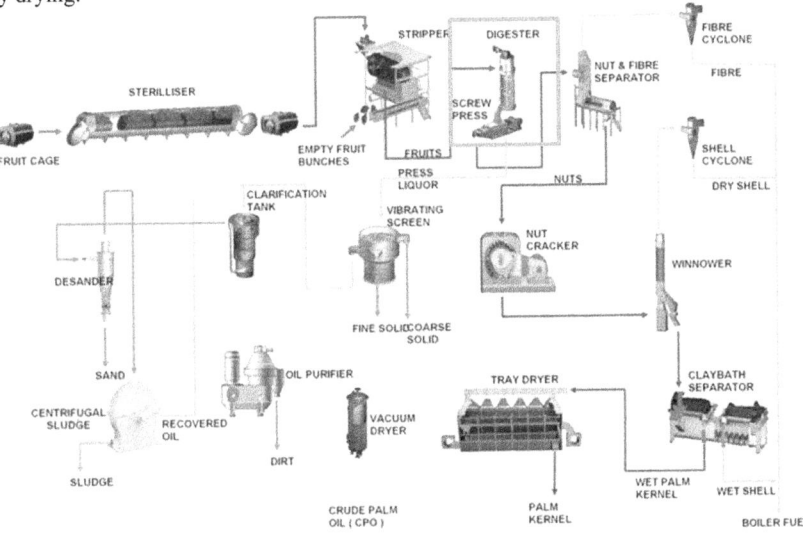

Fig. 9. Palm oil mill process flow diagram

4.1.2. CONVERSION OF PALM OIL TO BIODIESEL

The transesterification reaction is carried out with an alcohol excess (i.e. more alcohol than the stoichiometry would require). Typically the reaction is carried out at moderate temperature (up to 60 oC) and with residence times of 1-4 h. The catalyst is usually

NaOH (sodium hydroxide) or KOH (potassium hydroxide). After the reaction, we have a mixture of esters, glycerol, residual methanol and catalyst. Glycerol has very low solubility in the esters, therefore there will be two phases, which will be easily separable by sedimentation. Methanol will be present in both the biodiesel and (mainly) in the glycerol phase but is removed from the esters using distillation/evaporation and it is recycled to the start of the process. After methanol removal, the esters are purified by washing with acidic water to neutralise and remove any residual catalyst (NaOH or KOH, basic substances). Finally, any residual water is removed by drying.

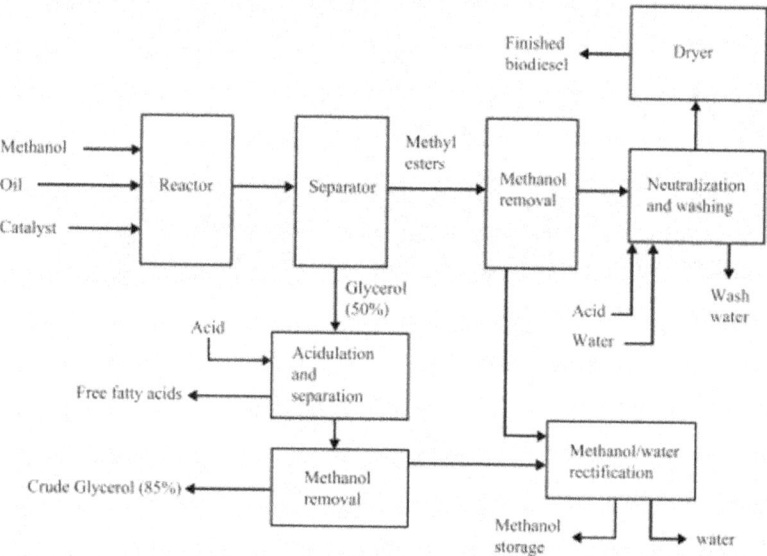

Fig. 2. Process flow schematic for biodiesel production.

Fig. 10. Process flow scheme for biodiesel production

A major problem to be considered is the use of fertile land to produce biofuel over food. This land could be used to grow food, therefore there is the risk of a food vs fuel competition (similar to the issue of bioethanol production from food crops). This is the main issue with biodiesel production from virgin vegetable oils. Thus, instead of Virgin Vegetable Oils, Waste Vegetable Oils is a more suitable biomass source for the production of biodiesel. Waste vegetable oil is collected and needs to be purified to remove any residuals from cooking and any residual water. Purification is obtained by screening (to remove large solid particles) and by sedimentation to remove water. After purification, vegetable oil can be converted to biodiesel using the same processes (transesterification reaction, glycerol separation and purification) used for biodiesel production from virgin oils.

5. IMPORTANT FACTORS TO CONSIDER IN THE PRODUCTION OF BIOFUELS AND BIOENERGY

5.1. FEEDSTOCK CONSIDERATIONS

Feedstock selection significantly impacts the process scheme configuration and reliability/ maintainability of a conversion plant. The low sulphur content of biomass and its lower carbon footprint than fossil alternatives has led to considerable interest in thermo-chemical conversion of biomass over co-conversion with coal or oil to reduce the environmental impact of fossil fuel use. However, it should be realised that the fundamentally different chemical composition of the feedstocks and their combination may result in constraints on conversion plant design or operation, ultimately impacting GHG emissions and the production efficiency of the syngas or liquid fuels and consequently its end utilisation. For example, combustion of waste material is often carried out at lower steam temperatures to avoid boiler corrosion and fouling; gasification of woody biomass produces a syngas with significant quantities of tar that must be removed or converted to avoid damage to downstream conversion plant and liquid bio-oil must be deoxygenated to be used satisfactorily in conventional combustion engines and trace impurities removed prior to successful catalytic conversion.

5.2. SCALE OF OPERATION

It is also important to consider scale of operation. Biomass conversion plants are often much smaller than traditional fossil fuel-fired facilities owing to the level of local feedstock availability. For example, many downdraft gasifiers or small scale pyrolysis units operate in rural areas, often on locally sourced feedstock from farms. The choice of the most appropriate technology for a bioenergy development is driven by a range of factors: available feedstock and its properties, scale of operation, and desired energy endvector. This results in different technologies having different market niches, e.g. use of pyrolysis to overcome logistic costs with small units providing a liquid fuel input to larger scale upgrading facilities to transport fuels, small-medium scale gasification for gas grid injection or CHP, and large-scale waste combustion for power or CHP.

It is important to note that combustion efficiency and control of airborne pollutants and unburned carbon are usually improved at larger scales. Gas engines and internal combustion engines are reasonably insensitive to variations in scale. However, steam turbines and steam cycles achieve very much higher efficiencies at higher steam conditions and so generally higher efficiencies are achieved at larger scales.

5.3. PRE-PROCESSING TECHNOLOGIES

Different conversion processes require different feedstock pre-processing. Downdraft gasifiers can operate with chipped or pelletised solid fuels, fluidised beds require fairly consistently sized feedstocks, and feedstocks for entrained flow gasifiers generally need to be ground or slurried, depending on the gasifier type. This places different demands on resources. The energy requirements are substantially greater for producing powders or submillimetre particulates than for larger chipped size feedstock.

Pelletising may offer some advantages as it results in a homogenised, uniform feedstock, improving process controllability (a particular advantage for waste and refuse-derived feedstocks, with high levels of feedstock variability). Pelletising may also minimise feedstock losses during storage and pellets can sometimes be conveniently integrated into existing fossil fuel infrastructure (e.g. co-firing in mills at large coal-fired utility plants). However, pelletising requires drying, grinding, and pressing of the material, exerting sufficient pressure to melt the lignin in the wood. Sometimes a binder may also be added to improve pellet physical properties. After pelletising, the feedstock should be more robust to mechanical handling, resulting in lower levels of losses along the supply chain.

5.4. CONCLUSION

Overall the conversion technology choice should be based on the feedstock available, its composition, and the required end use. LCA and techno-economic assessments can be utilised to optimise the economics and maximise GHG savings.

www.ingramcontent.com/pod-product-compliance
Lightning Source LLC
Chambersburg PA
CBHW072057230526
45479CB00010B/1119